THIS BOOK
BELONGS TO:

If you are a social worker, you don't need anybody to explain how important your job is, how significant your impact can be, and how necessary your career has become nowadays.

You are buying this book precisely to unplug from what has been said above.

This coloring book is suitable for work, meaning that there is no swearing in it. You will be able to have it with you at all times if that is what you want.

It has lots of space to color. And all the quotes inside aim to make you laugh or roll your eyes. Sometimes you might even feel embarrassed to agree with them. In the end, the idea is just to give you a great excuse to gift your brain with a well-deserved break.

Get joy while coloring. Feel free to hang your pages around when they are complete. Just maybe, not right at the office where you attend your clients... wink wink.

Now, have fun coloring, and be welcome to always come for more (click on brand name to find more books).

Let's rock the colorful life of a social worker!

SOCIAL WORK
COLORFUL
LIFE

I FINISHED COLORING THIS PAGE ON THIS DATE:

____

Today's forecast:
mostly paperworky
with 90% chance
of angry people

I FINISHED COLORING THIS PAGE ON THIS DATE:

____

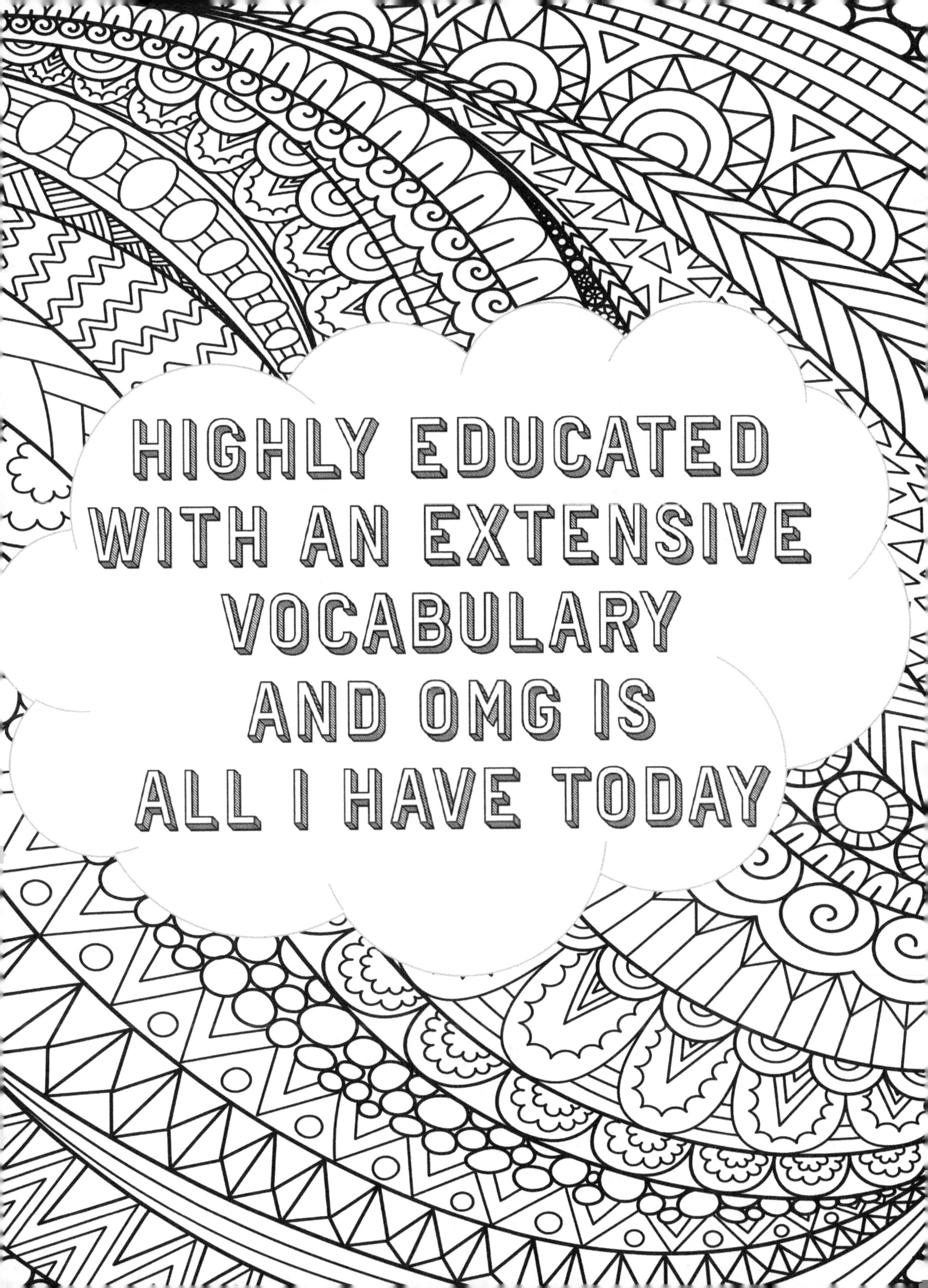

HIGHLY EDUCATED
WITH AN EXTENSIVE
VOCABULARY
AND OMG IS
ALL I HAVE TODAY

I FINISHED COLORING THIS PAGE ON THIS DATE:

____

Daily choice:
lunch break
or
social work

I FINISHED COLORING THIS PAGE ON THIS DATE:

____

SOCIAL WORKERS
DON'T GET DRUNK.
EVER.
THEY JUST ENHANCE
THEIR CURRENT LIFE.

I FINISHED COLORING THIS PAGE ON THIS DATE:

____

Social Worker
by day.
Really tired
by night.

I FINISHED COLORING THIS PAGE ON THIS DATE:

____

SAVING THE WORLD
ONE PROGRESS NOTE
AT A TIME

I FINISHED COLORING THIS PAGE ON THIS DATE:

____

I don't need to
write it down.
I'll remember it.
Yeah, right, sure...

I FINISHED COLORING THIS PAGE ON THIS DATE:

____

IDENTIFY THE PROBLEM
FIX IT
PICK UP THE PHONE
REPEAT

I FINISHED COLORING THIS PAGE ON THIS DATE:

____

I don't criticize
people's bad habits.
I mostly envy them all.

I FINISHED COLORING THIS PAGE ON THIS DATE:

____

SOCIAL WORKER:
A BROWSER WITH
2946 TABS OPEN
ALL. THE. TIME.

I FINISHED COLORING THIS PAGE ON THIS DATE:

____

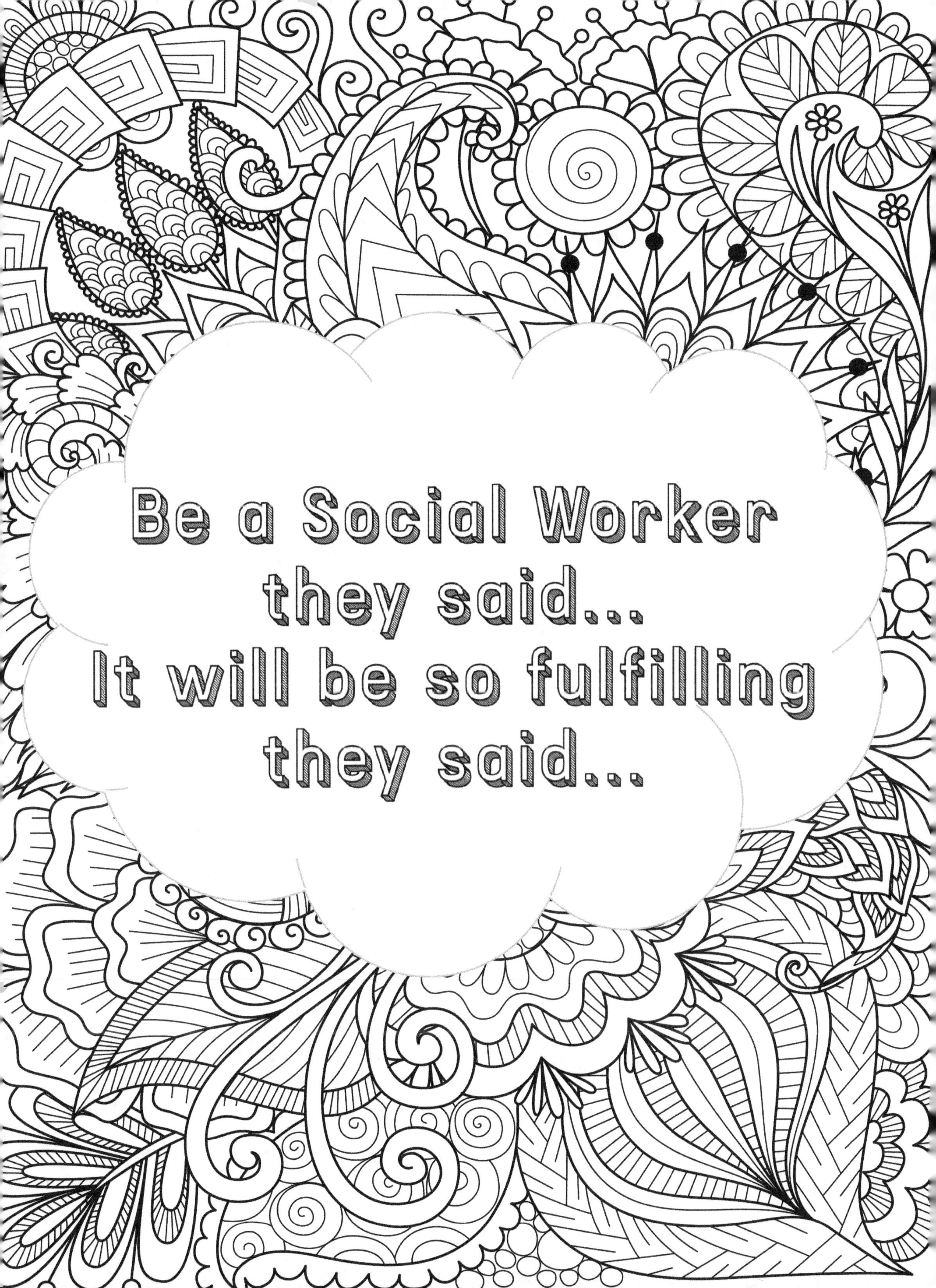
Be a Social Worker
they said...
It will be so fulfilling
they said...

I FINISHED COLORING THIS PAGE ON THIS DATE:

____

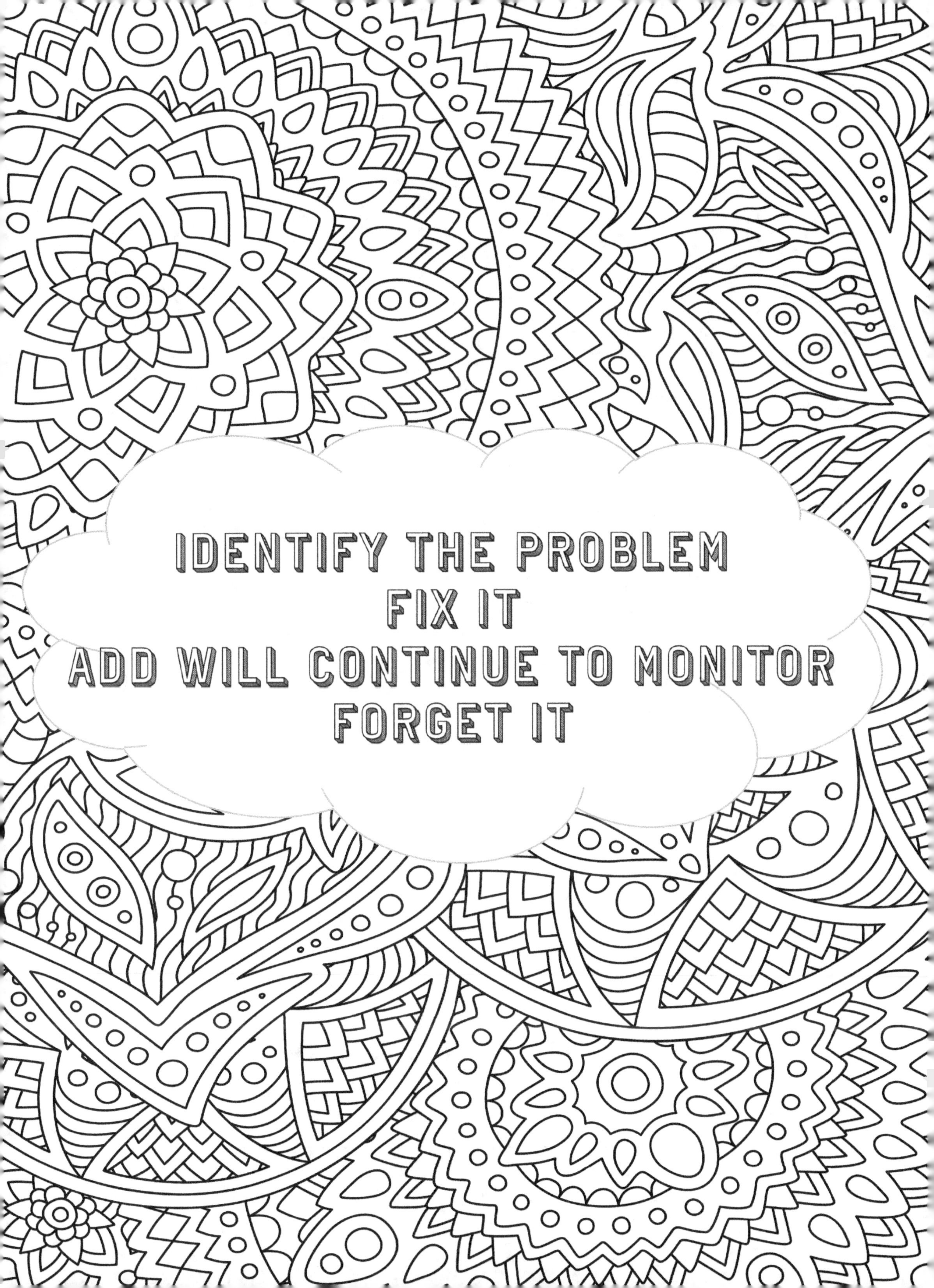
IDENTIFY THE PROBLEM
FIX IT
ADD WILL CONTINUE TO MONITOR
FORGET IT

I FINISHED COLORING THIS PAGE ON THIS DATE:

____

40 hours work
week:
my first
part time job.

I FINISHED COLORING THIS PAGE ON THIS DATE:

____

THE WORST NIGHTMARE:
MY CASE NOTES
AREN'T UP TO DATE

I FINISHED COLORING THIS PAGE ON THIS DATE:

____

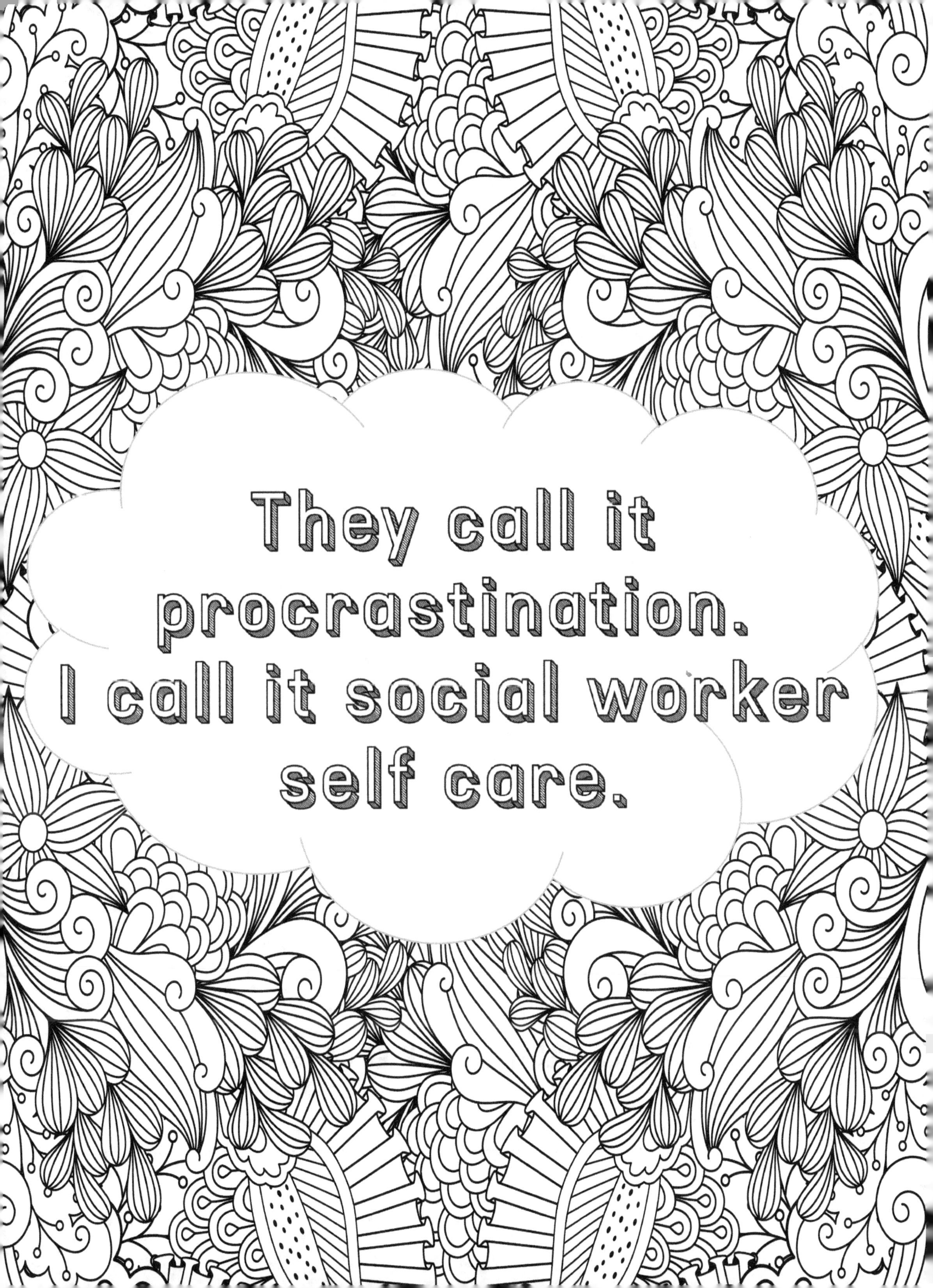

They call it
procrastination.
I call it social worker
self care.

I FINISHED COLORING THIS PAGE ON THIS DATE:

____

SEEING A CLIENT
OUT IN PUBLIC:
HIDE YOUR DRINK!
HIDE YOURSELF!

I FINISHED COLORING THIS PAGE ON THIS DATE:

____

Studied Social Work
to save the world.
Now I can't barely
save myself.

I FINISHED COLORING THIS PAGE ON THIS DATE:

____

ENJOY THOSE BITS
OF CALMNESS
PAPERWORK
IS COMING

I FINISHED COLORING THIS PAGE ON THIS DATE:

____

When you need
a motivational
interview technique
and all you have is
"I feel you"

I FINISHED COLORING THIS PAGE ON THIS DATE:

____

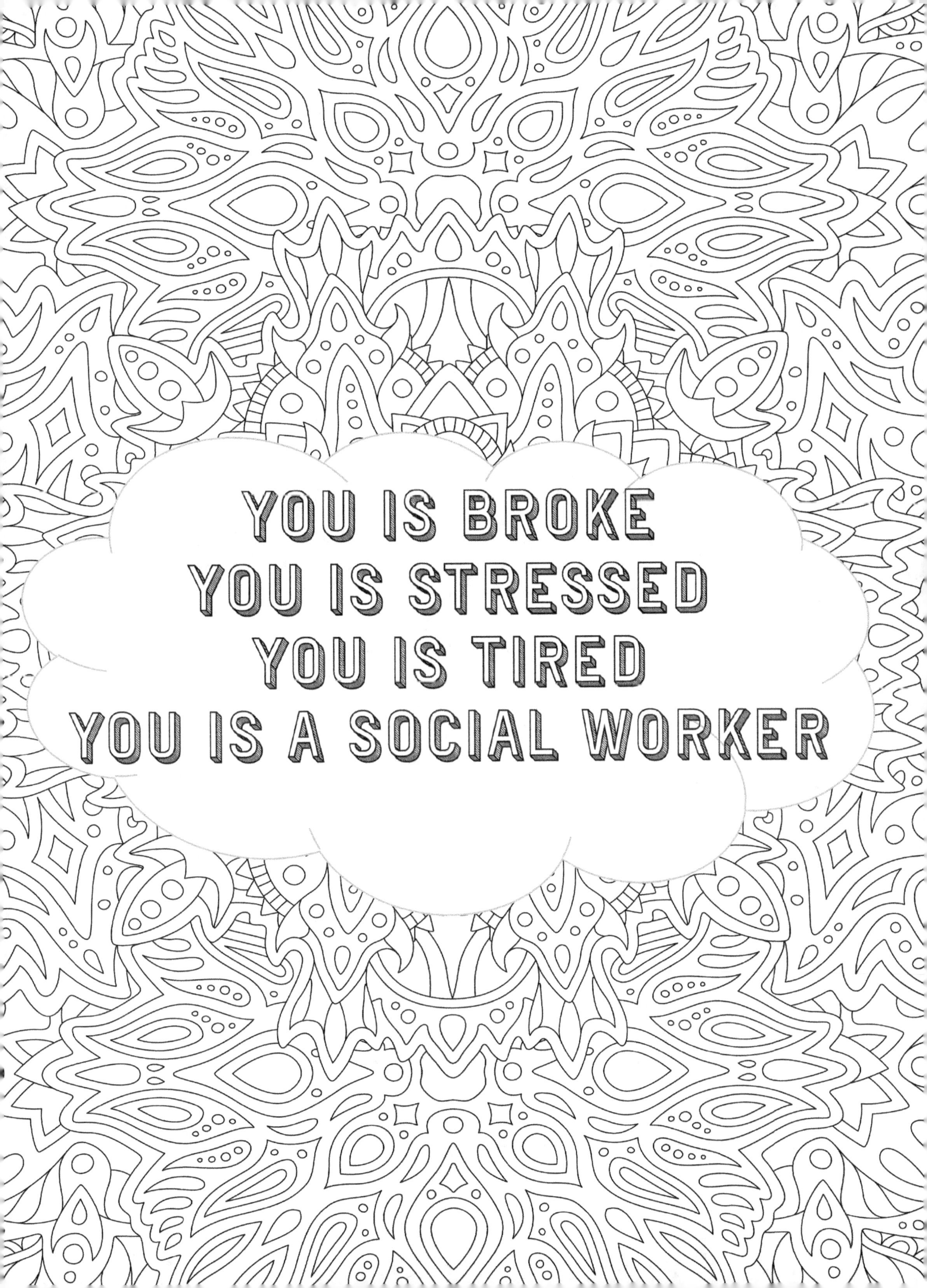

YOU IS BROKE
YOU IS STRESSED
YOU IS TIRED
YOU IS A SOCIAL WORKER

I FINISHED COLORING THIS PAGE ON THIS DATE:

____

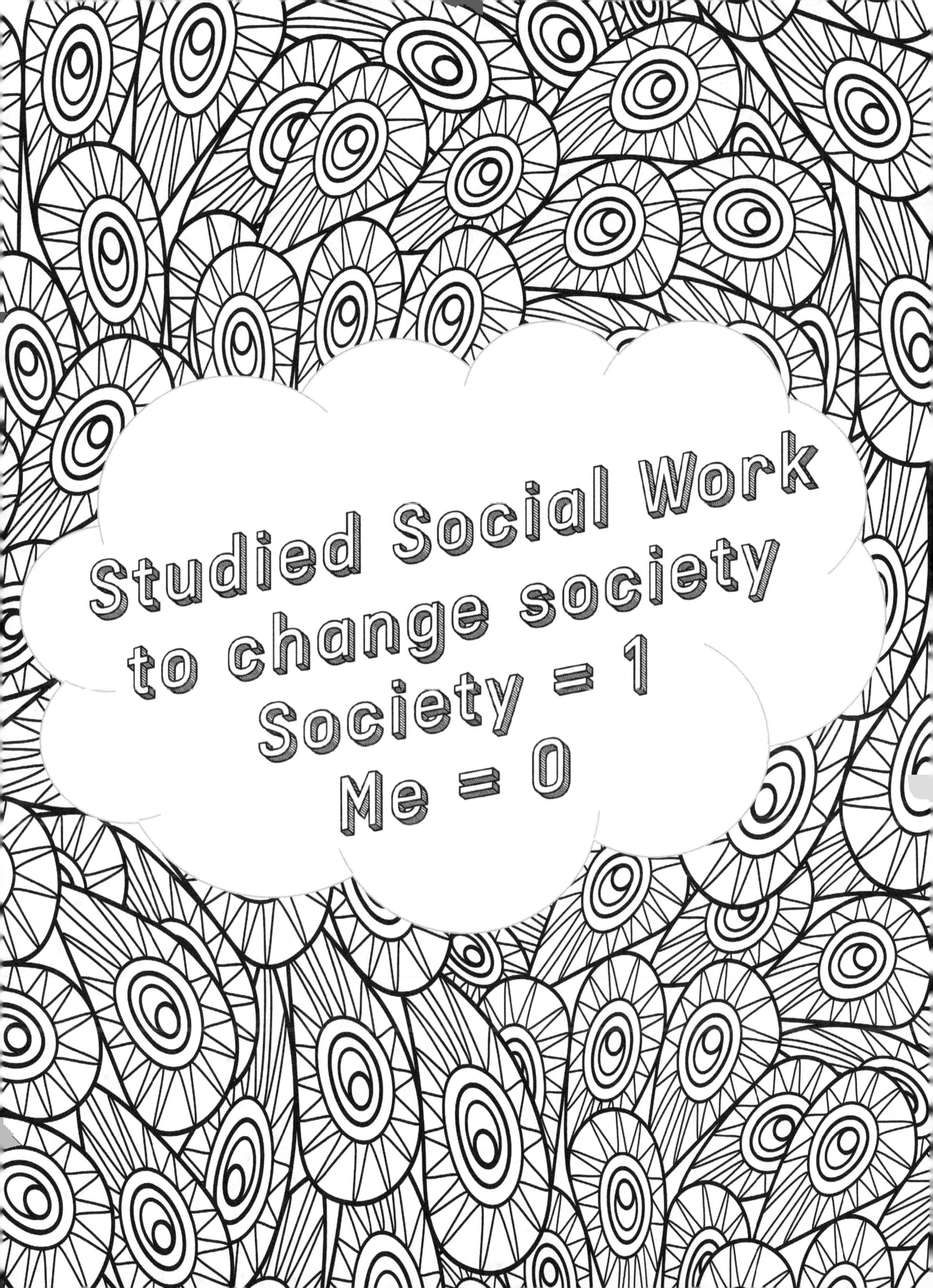

Studied Social Work
to change society
Society = 1
Me = 0

I FINISHED COLORING THIS PAGE ON THIS DATE:

____

I DON'T CALL IT
STRESS
I CALL IT
SOCIAL WORK

I FINISHED COLORING THIS PAGE ON THIS DATE:

____

Clients are convinced
that every
social worker's life
is problem free

I FINISHED COLORING THIS PAGE ON THIS DATE:

____

TYPING UP
ASSESSMENTS
IS LONGER THAN
WORK DAYS

I FINISHED COLORING THIS PAGE ON THIS DATE:

____

Social Workers never complain but we do wine!

I FINISHED COLORING THIS PAGE ON THIS DATE:

____

COMING BACK FROM
HOLIDAYS
AND SEEING
THE UNREAD MAIL:
"WHY DIDN'T I
CALL SICK?"

I FINISHED COLORING THIS PAGE ON THIS DATE:

____

When your client tells you
that you can handle anything
and you are like
"Say what?"

I FINISHED COLORING THIS PAGE ON THIS DATE:

____

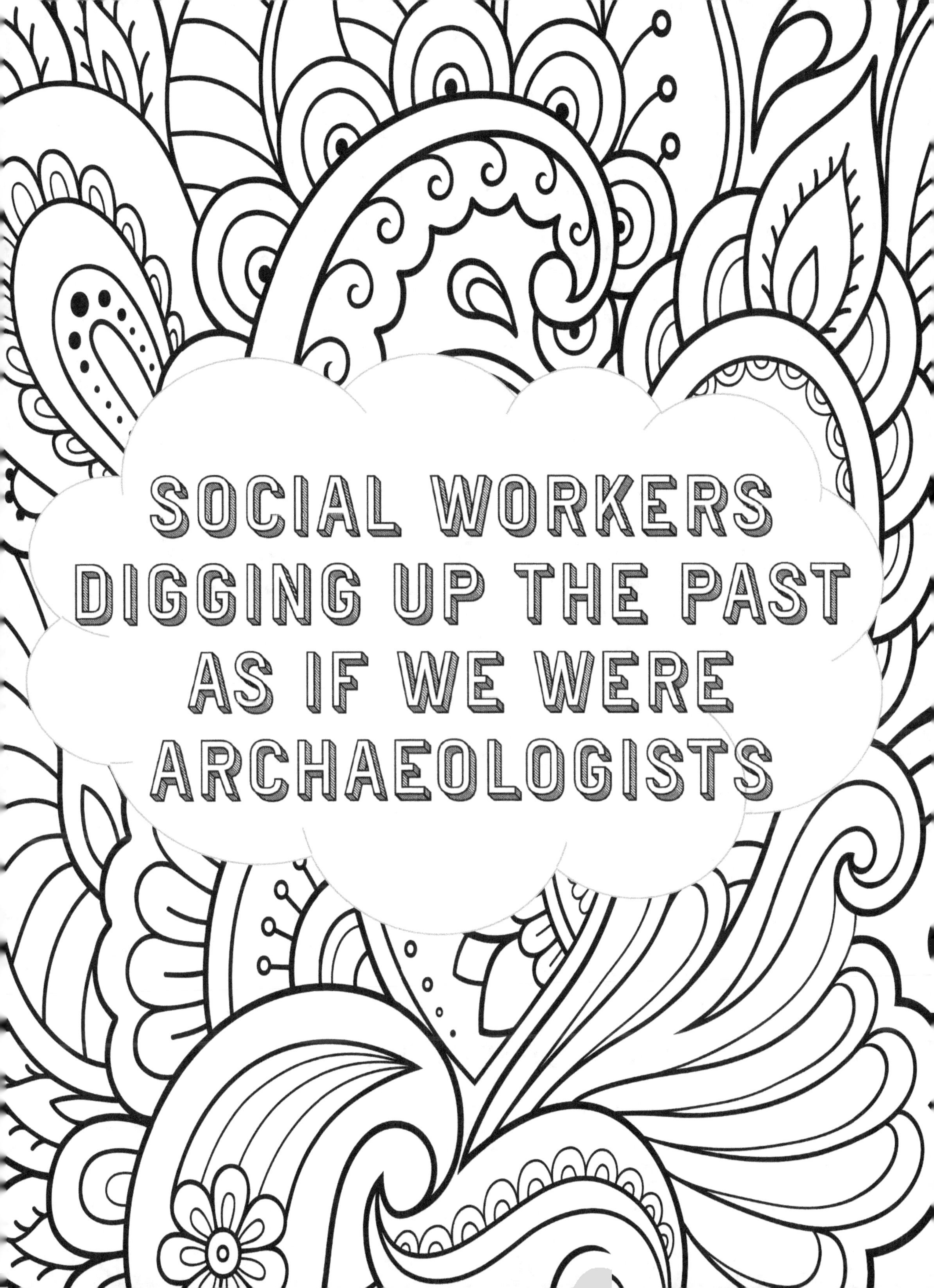

SOCIAL WORKERS
DIGGING UP THE PAST
AS IF WE WERE
ARCHAEOLOGISTS

I FINISHED COLORING THIS PAGE ON THIS DATE:

____

I chose my field
to help the
underprivileged.
Still waiting
for that help!

I FINISHED COLORING THIS PAGE ON THIS DATE:

____

NOBODY TOLD ME
THAT SOCIAL WORK
WAS A BAD IDEA.
NO FREAKING BODY!

I FINISHED COLORING THIS PAGE ON THIS DATE:

____

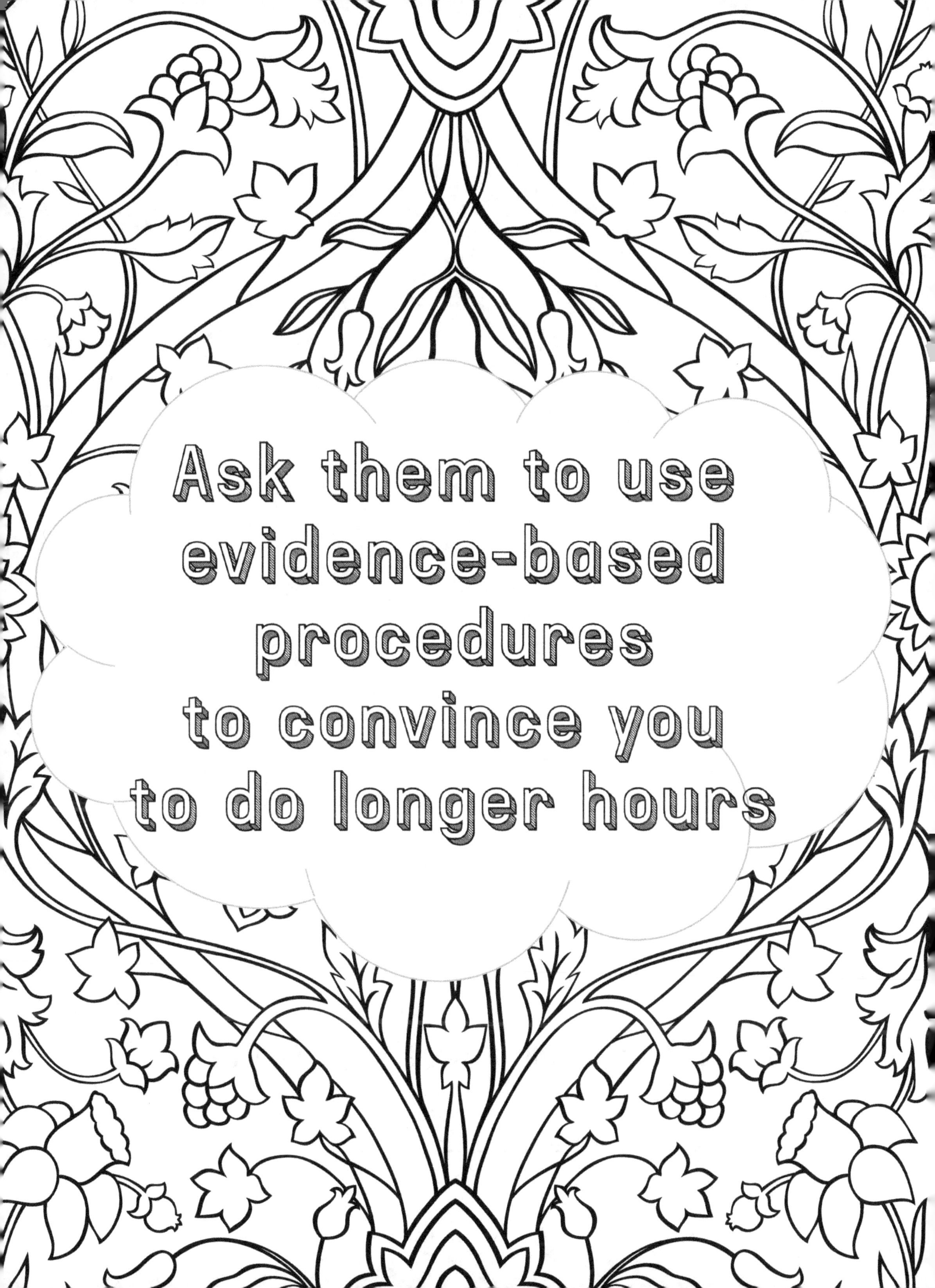

Ask them to use
evidence-based
procedures
to convince you
to do longer hours

I FINISHED COLORING THIS PAGE ON THIS DATE:

____

I CAN'T BELIEVE
I WORK THIS HARD
TO BE THIS POOR

I FINISHED COLORING THIS PAGE ON THIS DATE:

____

Let's celebrate social work
bring coffee,
chocolate,
antidepressants!

I FINISHED COLORING THIS PAGE ON THIS DATE:

____

I'M A SOCIAL WORKER
BURN OUT IS
MY STARTING POINT

I FINISHED COLORING THIS PAGE ON THIS DATE:

____

Social worker's
friday night plan:
stay home
drink wine
kill the phone

I FINISHED COLORING THIS PAGE ON THIS DATE:

____

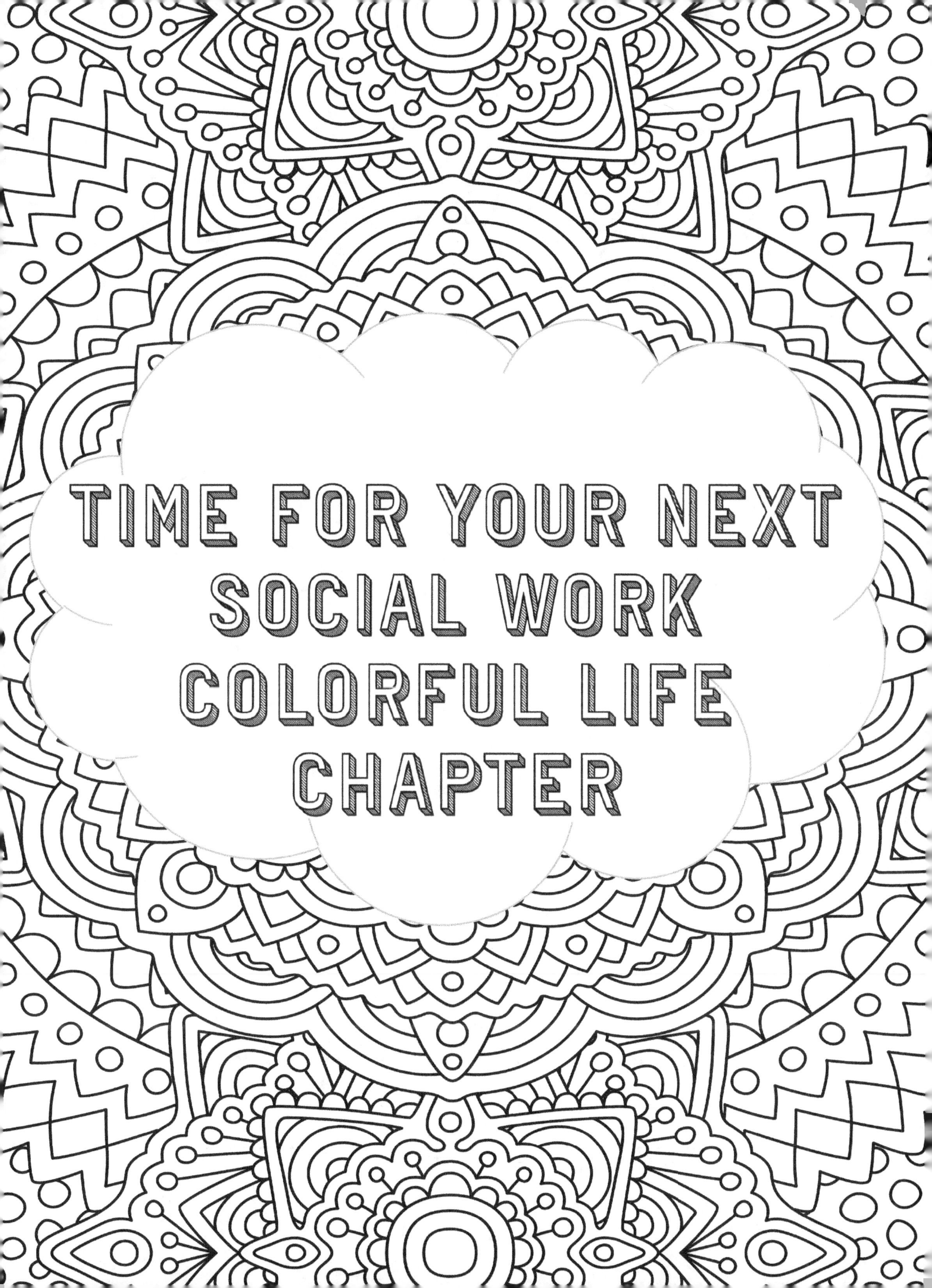
TIME FOR YOUR NEXT
SOCIAL WORK
COLORFUL LIFE
CHAPTER

I FINISHED COLORING THIS PAGE ON THIS DATE:

____

www.ingramcontent.com/pod-product-compliance
Lightning Source LLC
Chambersburg PA
CBHW080235260726
48658CB00008B/3099